Inkle and Yarico by George Colman the Younger

IØ163433

AN OPERA, IN THREE ACTS

AS PERFORMED AT THE THEATRES ROYAL COVENT GARDEN, AND HAYMARKET

George Colman the Younger was born on 21st October 1762, the son of George Colman the Elder, a noted and successful playwright and translator of Terence and Plautus among others.

Colman was educated at Westminster School before going on to University at Christ Church, Oxford, and then King's College, University of Aberdeen, before finally proceeding to Lincoln's Inn, London to become a student in Law.

In 1782 his first play 'The Female Dramatist' was premiered at his father's Haymarket theatre.

It appears that as early as 1784, Colman had entered into a runaway marriage with an actress, Clara Morris, to whose brother David Morris, he eventually sold his inherited share in the Haymarket theatre.

After her death he wrote many of the leading parts in his plays for Mrs Gibbs (née Logan), whom he was said to have secretly married after the death of his first wife.

His father, George Colman the Elder, was by now in failing health and was obliged to relinquish to his son the management of the Haymarket theatre in 1789, at a yearly salary of £600. Although Colman sought to emulate and build on the success of his father he was not quite of the same caliber.

On the death of his father in 1794, the Haymarket patent was continued to the son; but difficulties arose in his path, he was involved in litigation with Thomas Harris, and was unable to pay the running expenses of the performances at the Haymarket. In dire circumstances Colman was forced to seek sanctuary within the Rules of the King's Bench Prison. Although he would continue to manage the affairs of the theatre he would reside here for several years.

Released at last through the kindness of George IV, who had appointed him exon. of the Yeomen of the Guard, a dignity that Colman soon liquidated to the highest bidder.

In 1824 he was made examiner of plays by the Duke of Montrose, then the Lord Chamberlain. This granting of office caused widespread controversy amongst his peers who were appalled at his severe censorship and illiberal views, especially as his own works were often condemned as indecent. Apparently at times even the words 'heaven' and 'angel' were deemed to be offensive by him.

George Colman the Younger held this office until his death in Brompton, London on 17th October 1836 at the age of 73. He was buried alongside his father in Kensington Church.

Index of Contents

This is a drama, which might remove from Mr. Wilberforce his aversion to theatrical exhibitions, and convince him, that the teaching of moral duty is not confined to particular spots of ground; for, in those places, of all others, the doctrine is most effectually inculcated, where exhortation is the most required—the resorts of the gay, the idle, and the dissipated.

This opera was written, when the author was very young; and, should he live to be very old, he will have reason to be proud of it to his latest day— for it is one of those plays which is independent of time, of place, or of circumstance, for its value. It was popular before the subject of the abolition of the slave trade was popular. It has the peculiar honour of preceding that great question. It was the bright forerunner of alleviation to the hardships of slavery.

The trivial faults of this opera are—too much play on words (as it is called) by Trudge; and some classical allusions by other characters, in whose education such knowledge could not be an ingredient.

A fault more important, is—that the scene at the commencement of the opera, instead of Africa, is placed in America. It would undoubtedly have been a quick passage, to have crossed a fourth part of the western globe, during the interval between the first and second acts; still, as the hero and heroine of the drama were compelled to go to sea—imagination, with but little more exertion, might have given them a fair wind as well from the coast whence slaves are really brought, as from a shore where no such traffic is held.

As an opera, Inkle and Yarico has the singular merit not to be protected, though aided, by the power of music: the characters are so forcibly drawn, that even those performers who sing, and study that art alone, can render every part effectual: and singers and actors of future times, like those of the past, and of the present, will find every character exactly suited to their talents.

This opera has been performed in every London theatre, and in every theatre of the kingdom, with the same degree of splendid success. It would have been wonderful had its reception been otherwise; for the subject is a most interesting one, and in the treatment of it, the author has shewn taste, judgment—virtue.

No doubt the author would have ingenuity to argue away this objection—but that, which requires argument for its support in a dramatic work, is a subject for complaint. As slaves are imported from Africa, and never from America, the audience, in the two last acts of this play, feel as if they had been in the wrong quarter of the globe during the first act. Inkle could certainly steal a native from America, and sell her in Barbadoes, but this is not so consonant with that nice imitation of the order of things as to rank above criticism.

PERSONS REPRESENTED

COVENT GARDEN

Inkle	Mr. Johnstone.
Sir Christopher Curry	Mr. Quick.
Campley	Mr. Davies.
Medium	Mr. Wewitzer.
Trudge	Mr. Edwin.
Mate	Mr. Darley.
Yarico	Mrs. Billington.
Narcissa	Mrs. Mountain.
Wowski	Mrs. Martyr.
Patty	Mrs. Rock.

HAYMARKET

Inkle	Mr. Bannister, jun.
Sir Christopher Curry	Mr. Parsons.
Medium	Mr. Baddeley.
Campley	Mr. Davies.
Trudge	Mr. Edwin.
Mate	Mr. Meadows.
Yarico	Mrs. Kemble.
Narcissa	Mrs. Bannister.
Wowski	Miss George.
Patty	Mrs. Forster.

SCENE:—First on the Main of America: Afterwards in Barbadoes.

ACT THE FIRST

SCENE I

An American Forest

MEDIUM [Without]
Hilli ho! ho!

TRUDGE [Without]
Hip! hollo! ho!—Hip!—

[Enter **MEDIUM** and **TRUDGE**.

MEDIUM
Pshaw! it's only wasting time and breath. Bawling won't persuade him to budge a bit faster, and, whatever weight it may have in some places, bawling, it seems, don't go for argument here. Plague on't! we are now in the wilds of America.

TRUDGE
Hip, hillio—ho—hi!—

MEDIUM
Hold your tongue, you blockhead, or—

TRUDGE
Lord! sir, if my master makes no more haste, we shall all be put to sword by the knives of the natives. I'm told they take off heads like hats, and hang 'em on pegs, in their parlours. Mercy on us! My head aches with the very thoughts of it. Hollo! Mr. Inkle! master; hollo!

MEDIUM [Stops his mouth]
Head aches! Zounds, so does mine, with your confounded bawling. It's enough to bring all the natives about us; and we shall be stripped and plundered in a minute.

TRUDGE
Aye; stripping is the first thing that would happen to us; for they seem to be woefully off for a wardrobe. I myself saw three, at a distance, with less clothes than I have, when I get out of bed: all dancing about in black buff; just like Adam in mourning.

MEDIUM
This is to have to do with a schemer! a fellow who risks his life, for a chance of advancing his interest.—Always advantage in view! Trying, here, to make discoveries, that may promote his profit in England. Another Botany Bay scheme, mayhap. Nothing else could induce him to quit our foraging party, from the ship; when he knows every inhabitant here is not only as black as a pepper-corn, but as hot into the bargain— and I, like a fool, to follow him! and then to let him loiter behind.— [Calling]
—Why, nephew;—Why, Inkle.—

TRUDGE
Why, Inkle—Well! only to see the difference of men! he'd have thought it very hard, now, if I had let him call so often after me. Ah! I wish he was calling after me now, in the old jog-trot way, again. What a fool was I to leave London for foreign parts!—That ever I should leave Threadneedle-street, to thread an American forest, where a man's as soon lost as a needle in a bottle of hay!

MEDIUM
Patience, Trudge! Patience! If we once recover the ship—

TRUDGE
Lord, sir, I shall never recover what I have lost in coming abroad. When my master and I were in London, I had such a mortal snug birth of it! Why, I was factotum.

MEDIUM
Factotum to a young merchant is no such sinecure, neither.

TRUDGE

But then the honour of it. Think of that, sir; to be clerk as well as own man. Only consider. You find very few city clerks made out of a man, now-a-days. To be king of the counting-house, as well as lord of the bed-chamber. Ah! if I had him but now in the little dressing-room behind the office; tying his hair, with a bit of red tape, as usual.

MEDIUM

Yes, or writing an invoice in lampblack, and shining his shoes with an ink-bottle, as usual, you blundering blockhead!

TRUDGE

Oh, if I was but brushing the accounts or casting up the coats! mercy on us! what's that?

MEDIUM

That! What?

TRUDGE

Didn't you hear a noise?

MEDIUM

Y—es—but—hush! Oh, heavens be praised! here he is at last.

[Enter **INKLE**.

Now, nephew!

INKLE

So, Mr. Medium.

MEDIUM

Zounds, one would think, by your confounded composure, that you were walking in St. James's Park, instead of an American forest: and that all the beasts were nothing but good company. The hollow trees, here, sentry boxes, and the lions in 'em, soldiers; the jackalls, courtiers; the crocodiles, fine women; and the baboons, beaus. What the plague made you loiter so long?

INKLE
Reflection.

MEDIUM
So I should think; reflection generally comes lagging behind. What, scheming, I suppose; never quiet. At it again, eh? What a happy trader is your father, to have so prudent a son for a partner! Why, you are the carefullest Co. in the whole city. Never losing sight of the main chance; and that's the reason, perhaps, you lost sight of us, here, on the main of America.

INKLE
Right, Mr. Medium. Arithmetic, I own, has been the means of our parting at present.

TRUDGE [Aside]
Ha! A sum in division, I reckon.

MEDIUM
And pray, if I may be so bold, what mighty scheme has just tempted you to employ your head, when you ought to make use of your heels?

INKLE
My heels! Here's pretty doctrine! Do you think I travel merely for motion? What, would you have a man of business come abroad, scamper extravagantly here and there and every where, then return home, and have nothing to tell, but that he has been here and there and every where? 'Sdeath, sir, would you have me travel like a lord?

MEDIUM
No, the Lord forbid!

INKLE
Travelling, uncle, was always intended for improvement; and improvement is an advantage; and advantage is profit, and profit is gain. Which in the travelling translation of a trader, means, that you should gain every advantage of improving your profit. I have been comparing the land, here, with that of our own country.

MEDIUM

And you find it like a good deal of the land of our own country—cursedly encumbered with black legs, I take it.

INKLE
And calculating how much it might be made to produce by the acre.

MEDIUM
You were?

INKLE
Yes; I was proceeding algebraically upon the subject.

MEDIUM
Indeed!

INKLE
And just about extracting the square root.

MEDIUM
Hum!

INKLE
I was thinking too, if so many natives could be caught, how much they might fetch at the West Indian markets.

MEDIUM
Now let me ask you a question, or two, young cannibal catcher, if you please.

INKLE
Well.

MEDIUM
Ar'n't we bound for Barbadoes; partly to trade, but chiefly to carry home the daughter of the governor, Sir Christopher Curry, who has till now been under your father's care, in Threadneedle-street, for polite English education?

INKLE
Granted.

MEDIUM

And isn't it determined, between the old folks, that you are to marry Narcissa, as soon as we get there?

INKLE

A fixed thing.

MEDIUM

Then what the devil do you do here, hunting old hairy negroes, when you ought to be obliging a fine girl in the ship? Algebra, too! You'll have other things to think of when you are married, I promise you. A plodding fellow's head, in the hands of a young wife, like a boy's slate, after school, soon gets all its arithmetic wiped off: and then it appears in its true simple state: dark, empty, and bound in wood, Master Inkle.

INKLE

Not in a match of this kind. Why, it's a table of interest from beginning to end, old Medium.

MEDIUM

Well, well, this is no time to talk. Who knows but, instead of sailing to a wedding, we may get cut up, here, for a wedding dinner: tossed up for a dingy duke, perhaps, or stewed down for a black baronet, or eat raw by an inky commoner?

INKLE

Why sure you ar'n't afraid?

MEDIUM

Who, I afraid? Ha! ha! ha! No, not I! What the deuce should I be afraid of? Thank Heaven I have a clear conscience, and need not be afraid of any thing. A scoundrel might not be quite so easy on such an occasion; but it's the part of an honest man not to behave like a scoundrel: I never behaved like a scoundrel—for which reason I am an honest man, you know. But come—I hate to boast of my good qualities.

INKLE

Slow and sure, my good, virtuous Mr. Medium! Our companions can be but half a mile before us: and, if we do but double their steps, we shall overtake 'em at one mile's end, by all the powers of arithmetic.

MEDIUM
Oh curse your arithmetic!

[Exeunt.

SCENE II

Another part of the Forest

A ship at anchor in the bay at a small distance.—Mouth of a cave.

Enter **SAILORS** and **MATE**, as returning from foraging.

MATE
Come, come, bear a hand, my lads. Tho'f the bay is just under our bowsprits, it will take a damned deal of tripping to come at it—there's hardly any steering clear of the rocks here. But do we muster all hands? All right, think ye?

1st SAILOR
All to a man—besides yourself, and a monkey—the three land lubbers, that edged away in the morning, goes for nothing, you know—they're all dead, may-hap, by this.

MATE
Dead! you be—Why they're friends of the captain; and if not brought safe aboard to-night, you may all chance to have a salt eel for your supper— that's all—Moreover the young plodding spark, he with the grave, foul weather face, there, is to man the tight little frigate, Miss Narcissa—what d'ye call her? that is bound with us for Barbadoes. Rot'em for not keeping under weigh, I say! But come, let's see if a song will bring 'em too. Let's have a full chorus to the good merchant ship, the Achilles, that's wrote by our captain.

SONG.

The Achilles, though christen'd, good ship, 'tis surmis'd,
From that old man of war, great Achilles, so priz'd,
Was he, like our vessel, pray fairly baptiz'd?
Ti tol lol, &c.

Poets sung that Achilles—if, now, they've an itch
To sing this, future ages may know which is which;
And that one rode in Greece—and the other in pitch.
Ti tol lol, &c.

What tho' but a merchant ship—sure our supplies:
Now your men of war's gain in a lottery lies,
And how blank they all look, when they can't get a prize!
Ti tol lol, &c.

What are all their fine names? when no rhino's behind,
The Intrepid, and Lion, look sheepish you'll find;
Whilst, alas! the poor Æolus can't raise the wind!
Ti tol lol, &c.

Then the Thunderer's dumb; out of tune the Orpheus;
The Ceres has nothing at all to produce;
And the Eagle I warrant you, looks like a goose.
Ti tol lol, &c.

1st SAILOR
Avast! look a-head there. Here they come, chased by a fleet of black devils.

MIDSHIPMAN
And the devil a fire have I to give them. We han't a grain of powder left. What must we do, lads?

2nd SAILOR
Do? Sheer off to be sure.

MIDSHIPMAN [Reluctantly]
Well, if I must, I must.

[Going to the other side, and holloing to **INKLE**, &c.

Yoho, lubbers! Crowd all the sail you can, d'ye mind me!

[Exeunt **SAILORS**.

[Enter **MEDIUM**, running across the stage, as pursued by the **BLACKS**.

MEDIUM
Nephew! Trudge! run—scamper! Scour—fly! Zounds, what harm did I
ever do to be hunted to death by a pack of bloodhounds? Why nephew!
Oh, confound your long sums in arithmetic! I'll take care of myself; and if
we must have any arithmetic, dot and carry one for my money.

[Runs off.

[Enter **INKLE** and **TRUDGE**, hastily.

TRUDGE
Oh! that ever I was born, to leave pen, ink, and powder for this!

INKLE
Trudge, how far are the sailors before us?

TRUDGE
I'll run and see, sir, directly.

INKLE
Blockhead, come here. The savages are close upon us; we shall scarce be
able to recover our party. Get behind this tuft of trees with me; they'll
pass us, and we may then recover our ship with safety.

TRUDGE [Going behind]
Oh! Threadneedle-street, Thread—

INKLE
Peace.

TRUDGE [Hiding]
—Needle-street.

[They hide behind trees. **NATIVES** cross. After a long pause, **INKLE** looks from the trees.

INKLE
Trudge.

TRUDGE [In a whisper]
Sir.

INKLE
Are they all gone by?

TRUDGE
Won't you look and see?

INKLE [Looking round]
So all is safe at last.

[Coming forward.

Nothing like policy in these cases; but you'd have run on, like a booby! A tree, I fancy, you'll find, in future, the best resource in a hot pursuit.

TRUDGE
Oh, charming! It's a retreat for a king, sir: Mr. Medium, however, has not got up in it; your uncle, sir, has run on like a booby; and has got up with our party by this time, I take it; who are now most likely at the shore. But what are we to do next, sir?

INKLE
Reconnoitre a little, and then proceed.

TRUDGE
Then pray, sir, proceed to reconnoitre; for the sooner the better.

INKLE
Then look out, d'ye hear, and tell me if you discover any danger.

TRUDGE

Y—Ye—s—Yes.

INKLE
Well, is the coast clear?

TRUDGE
Eh! Oh lord!—Clear!

[Rubbing his eyes.

Oh dear! oh dear! the coast will soon be clear enough now, I promise you—The ship is under sail, sir!

INKLE
Confusion! my property carried off in the vessel.

TRUDGE
All, all, sir, except me.

INKLE
They may report me dead, perhaps, and dispose of my property at the next island.

[The vessel appears under sail.

TRUDGE
Ah! there they go.

[A gun fired.

—That will be the last report we shall ever hear from 'em I'm afraid.—That's as much as to say, Good bye to ye. And here we are left—two fine, full-grown babes in the wood!

INKLE
What an ill-timed accident! Just too, when my speedy union with Narcissa, at Barbadoes, would so much advance my interests.—Ah, my Narcissa, I never shall forget thy last adieu.—Something must be hit upon, and speedily; but what resource?

TRUDGE

The old one—a tree, sir.—'Tis all we have for it now. What would I give, now, to be perched upon a high stool, with our brown desk squeezed into the pit of my stomach—scribbling away an old parchment!—But all my red ink will be spilt by an old black pin of a negro.

SONG.

[Last Valentine's Day]

A voyage over seas had not entered my head,
Had I known but on which side to butter my bread,
Heigho! sure I—for hunger must die!
I've sail'd like a booby; come here in a squall,
Where, alas! there's no bread to be butter'd at all!
Oho! I'm a terrible booby!
Oh, what a sad booby am I!
In London, what gay chop-house signs in the street!
But the only sign here is of nothing to eat.
Heigho! that I—for hunger should die!
My mutton's all lost; I'm a poor starving elf!
And for all the world like a lost mutton myself.
Oho! I shall die a lost mutton!
Oh! what a lost mutton am I!
For a neat slice of beef, I could roar like a bull;
And my stomach's so empty, my heart is quite full.
Heigho! that I—for hunger should die!
But, grave without meat, I must here meet my grave,
For my bacon, I fancy, I never shall save.
Oho! I shall ne'er save my bacon!
I can't save my bacon, not I!

TRUDGE

Hum! I was thinking—I was thinking, sir—if so many natives could be caught, how much they might fetch at the West India markets!

INKLE

Scoundrel! is this a time to jest?

TRUDGE

No, faith, sir! Hunger is too sharp to be jested with. As for me, I shall starve for want of food. Now you may meet a luckier fate: you are able to extract the square root, sir; and that's the very best provision you can find here to live upon. But I!

[Noise at a distance.

Mercy on us! here they come again.

INKLE
Confusion! Deserted on one side, and pressed on the other, which way shall I turn?—This cavern may prove a safe retreat to us for the present. I'll enter, cost what it will.

TRUDGE
Oh Lord! no, don't, don't—We shall pay too dear for our lodging, depend on't.

INKLE
This is no time for debating. You are at the mouth of it: lead the way, Trudge.

TRUDGE [Aside]
What! go in before your honour! I know my place better, I assure you—I might walk into more mouths than one, perhaps.

INKLE
Coward! then follow me.

[Noise again.

TRUDGE
I must, sir; I must! Ah, Trudge, Trudge! what a damned hole are you getting into!

[Exeunt into a Cavern.

.

SCENE III

A cave, decorated with skins of wild beasts, feathers, &c.

In the middle of the scene, a rude kind of curtain, by way of door to an inner apartment.

Enter **INKLE** and **TRUDGE**, as from the mouth of the cavern.

INKLE
So far, at least, we have proceeded with safety. Ha! no bad specimen of savage elegance. These ornaments would be worth something in England.—We have little to fear here, I hope: this cave rather bears the pleasing face of a profitable adventure.

TRUDGE
Very likely, sir! But for a pleasing face, it has the cursed'st ugly month I ever saw in my life. Now do, sir, make off as fast as you can. If we once get clear of the natives' houses, we have little to fear from the lions and leopards: for by the appearance of their parlours, they seem to have killed all the wild beast in the country. Now pray, do, my good master, take my advice, and run away.

INKLE
Rascal! Talk again of going out, and I'll flea you alive.

TRUDGE
That's just what I expect for coming in.—All that enter here appear to have had their skins stript over their ears; and ours will be kept for curiosities—We shall stand here, stuffed, for a couple of white wonders.

INKLE
This curtain seems to lead to another apartment: I'll draw it.

TRUDGE
No, no, no, don't; don't. We may be called to account for disturbing the company: you may get a curtain-lecture, perhaps, sir.

INKLE
Peace, booby, and stand on your guard.

TRUDGE
Oh! what will become of us! Some grim, seven foot fellow ready to scalp us.

INKLE
By heaven! a woman.

[As the curtain draws, **YARICO** and **WOWSKI** discovered asleep.

TRUDGE
A woman!
[Aside]—[Loud]
But let him come on; I'm ready—dam'me, I don't fear facing the devil himself—Faith it is a woman—fast asleep too.

INKLE
And beautiful as an angel!

TRUDGE
And egad! there seems to be a nice, little plump bit in the corner; only she's an angel of rather a darker sort.

INKLE
Hush! keep back—she wakes.

[**YARICO** comes forward—**INKLE** and **TRUDGE** retire to opposite sides of the scene.

SONG.—YARICO.
When the chace of day is done,
And the shaggy lion's skin,
Which for us, our warriors win,
Decks our cells at set of sun;
Worn with toil, with slap opprest,
I press my mossy bed, and sink to rest.
Then, once more, I see our train,
With all our chase renew'd again:
Once more 'tis day,
Once more our prey
Gnashes his angry teeth, and foams in vain.

Again, in sullen haste, he flies,
Ta'en in the toil, again he lies,
Again he roars—and, in my slumbers, dies.
Inkle and Trudge come forward.

INKLE
Our language!

TRUDGE
Zounds, she has thrown me into a cold sweat.

YARICO
Hark! I heard a noise! Wowski, awake! whence can it proceed?

[She awakes **WOWSKI**, and they both come forward—**YARICO** towards **INKLE**; **WOWSKI** towards **TRUDGE**.

YARICO
Ah! what form is this?—are you a man?

INKLE
True flesh and blood, my charming heathen, I promise you.

YARICO [Gazing]
What harmony in his voice! What a shape! How fair his skin too—.

TRUDGE
This must be a lady of quality, by her staring.

YARICO
Say, stranger, whence come you?

INKLE
From a far distant island; driven on this coast by distress, and deserted by my companions.

YARICO
And do you know the danger that surrounds you here? Our woods are filled with beasts of prey—my countrymen too—(yet, I think they cou'd'nt

find the heart)—might kill you.—It would be a pity if you fell in their way—I think I should weep if you came to any harm.

TRUDGE
O ho! It's time, I see, to begin making interest with the chamber maid.

[Takes **WOWSKI** apart.

INKLE
How wild and beautiful! sure there is magic in her shape, and she has rivetted me to the place. But where shall I look for safety? let me fly and avoid my death.

YARICO
Oh! no—don't depart.—But I will try to preserve you; and if you are killed, Yarico must die too! Yet, 'tis I alone can save you; your death is certain, without my assistance; and, indeed, indeed you shall not want it.

INKLE
My kind Yarico! what means, then, must be used for my safety?

YARICO
My cave must conceal you: none enter it, since my father was slain in battle. I will bring you food by day, then lead you to our unfrequented groves by moonlight, to listen to the nightingale. If you should sleep, I'll watch you, and awake you when there's danger.

INKLE
Generous maid! Then, to you will I owe my life; and whilst it lasts, nothing shall part us.

YARICO
And shan't it, shan't it indeed?

INKLE
No, my Yarico! For when an opportunity offers to return to my country, you shall be my companion.

YARICO
What! cross the seas!

INKLE

Yes, Help me to discover a vessel, and you shall enjoy wonders. You shall be decked in silks, my brave maid, and have a house drawn with horses to carry you.

YARICO

Nay, do not laugh at me—but is it so?

INKLE

It is indeed!

YARICO

Oh wonder! I wish my countrywomen could see me—But won't your warriors kill us?

INKLE

No, our only danger on land is here.

YARICO

Then let us retire further into the cave. Come—your safety is in my keeping.

INKLE

I follow you—Yet, can you run some risk in following me?

DUET.
[O say, Bonny Lass]

INKLE

O say, simple maid, have you form'd any notion
Of all the rude dangers in crossing the ocean?
When winds whistle shrilly, ah! won't they remind you,
To sigh with regret, for the grot left behind you?

YARICO

Ah! no, I could follow, and sail the world over,
Nor think of my grot, when I look at my lover;
The winds, which blow round us, your arms for my pillow,
Will lull us to sleep, whilst we're rocked by each billow.

BOTH
O say then my true love, we never will sunder,
Nor shrink from the tempest, nor dread the big thunder:
Whilst constant, we'll laugh at all changes of weather,
And journey all over the world both together.

[Exeunt; as retiring further into the cave.

[Manent **TRUDGE** and **WOWSKI**.

TRUDGE
Why, you speak English as well as I, my little Wowski.

WOWSKI
Iss.

TRUDGE
Iss! and you learnt it from a strange man, that tumbled from a big boat, many moons ago, you say?

WOWSKI
Iss—Teach me—teach good many.

TRUDGE
Then, what the devil made them so surprized at seeing us! was he like me?

[**WOWSKI** shakes her head.

Not so smart a body, mayhap. Was his face, now, round and comely, and—eh!

[Stroking his chin.

Was it like mine?

WOWSKI
Like dead leaf—brown and shrivel.

TRUDGE

Oh, oh, an old shipwrecked sailor, I warrant. With white and grey hair, eh, my pretty beauty spot?

WOWSKI

Iss; all white. When night come, he put it in pocket.

TRUDGE

Oh! wore a wig. But the old boy taught you something more than English, I believe.

WOWSKI

Iss.

TRUDGE

The devil he did! What was it?

WOWSKI

Teach me put dry grass, red hot, in hollow white stick.

TRUDGE

Aye, what was that for?

WOWSKI

Put in my mouth—go poff, poff!

TRUDGE

Zounds! did he teach you to smoke?

WOWSKI

Iss.

TRUDGE

And what became of him at last? What did your countrymen do for the poor fellow?

WOWSKI

Eat him one day—Our chief kill him.

TRUDGE

Mercy on us! what damned stomachs, to swallow a tough old tar! Ah, poor Trudge! your killing comes next.

WOWSKI
No, no—not you—no—

[Running to him anxiously.

TRUDGE
No? why what shall I do, if I get in their paws?

WOWSKI
I fight for you!

TRUDGE
Will you? Ecod she's a brave good-natured wench! she'll be worth a hundred of your English wives.—Whenever they fight on their husband's account, it's with him instead of for him, I fancy. But how the plague am I to live here?

WOWSKI
I feed you—bring you kid.

SONG.—WOWSKI.
[One day, I heard Mary say]
White man, never go away—
Tell me why need you?
Stay, with your Wowski, stay:
Wowski will feed you.
Cold moons are now coming in;
Ah, don't go grieve me!
I'll wrap you in leopard's skin:
White man, don't leave me.
And when all the sky is blue,
Sun makes warm weather,
I'll catch you a cockatoo,
Dress you in feather.
When cold comes, or when 'tis hot,
Ah, don't go grieve me!
Poor Wowski will be forgot—

White man, don't leave me!

TRUDGE
Zounds! leopard's skin for winter wear, and feathers for a summer's suit! Ha, ha! I shall look like a walking hammer-cloth, at Christmas, and an upright shuttlecock, in the dog days. And for all this, if my master and I find our way to England, you shall be part of our travelling equipage; and, when I get there, I'll give you a couple of snug rooms, on a first floor, and visit you every evening, as soon as I come from the counting-house. Do you like it?

WOWSKI
Iss.

TRUDGE
Damme, what a flashy fellow I shall seem in the city! I'll get her a white boy to bring up the tea-kettle. Then I'll teach you to write and dress hair.

WOWSKI
You great man in your country?

TRUDGE
Oh yes, a very great man. I'm head clerk of the counting-house, and first valet-de-chambre of the dressing-room. I pounce parchments, powder hair, black shoes, ink paper, shave beards, and mend pens. But hold! I had forgot one material point—you ar'n't married, I hope?

WOWSKI
No: you be my chum-chum!

TRUDGE
So I will. It's best, however, to be sure of her being single; for Indian husbands are not quite so complaisant as English ones, and the vulgar dogs might think of looking a little after their spouses. But you have had a lover or two in your time; eh, Wowski?

WOWSKI
Oh, iss—great many—I tell you.

DUET.

WOWSKI
Wampum, Swampum, Yanko, Lanko, Nanko, Pownatowski,
Black men—plenty—twenty—fight for me,
White man, woo you true?

TRUDGE
Who?

WOWSKI
You.

TRUDGE
Yes, pretty little Wowski!

WOWSKI
Then I leave all, and follow thee.

TRUDGE
Oh then turn about, my little tawny tight one!
Don't you like me?

WOWSKI
Iss, you're like the snow!
If you slight one—

TRUDGE
Never, not for any white one;
You are beautiful as any sloe.

WOWSKI
Wars, jars, scars, can't expose ye,
In our grot—

TRUDGE
So snug and cosey!

WOWSKI
Flowers, neatly
Pick'd, shall sweetly
Make your bed.

TRUDGE
Coying, toying,
With a rosy
Posey,
When I'm dosey,
Bear-skin nightcaps too shall warm my head.

BOTH
Bearskin nightcaps, &c. &c.

ACT THE SECOND

SCENE I

The Quay at Barbadoes, with an Inn upon it

PEOPLE employed in unlading vessels, carrying bales of goods, &c.

Enter **SEVERAL PLANTERS**.

1st PLANTER
I saw her this morning, gentlemen, you may depend on't. My telescope never fails me. I popp'd upon her as I was taking a peep from my balcony. A brave tight ship, I tell you, bearing down directly for Barbadoes here.

2nd PLANTER
Ods, my life! rare news! We have not had a vessel arrive in our harbour these six weeks.

3rd PLANTER
And the last brought only Madam Narcissa, our Governor's daughter, from England; with a parcel of lazy, idle, white folks about her. Such cargoes will never do for our trade, neighbour.

2nd PLANTER

No, no; we want slaves. A terrible dearth of 'em in Barbadoes, lately! But your dingy passengers for my money. Give me a vessel like a collier, where all the lading tumbles out as black as my hat.

[To **1st PLANTER**]

But are you sure, now, you ar'n't mistaken?

1st PLANTER

Mistaken! 'sbud, do you doubt my glass? I can discover a gull by it six leagues off: I could see every thing as plain as if I was on board.

2nd PLANTER

Indeed! and what were her colours?

1st PLANTER

Um! why English—or Dutch—or French—I don't exactly remember.

2nd PLANTER

What were the sailors aboard?

1st PLANTER

Eh! why they were English too—or Dutch—or French—I can't perfectly recollect.

2nd PLANTER

Your glass, neighbour, is a little like a glass too much: it makes you forget every thing you ought to remember.

[Cry without, "A sail, a sail!"

1st PLANTER

Egad, but I'm right though. Now, gentlemen!

ALL

Aye, aye; the devil take the hindmost.

[Exeunt hastily.

[Enter **NARCISSA** and **PATTY**.

SONG

Freshly now the breeze is blowing,
As yon ship at anchor rides;
Sullen waves, incessant flowing,
Rudely dash against the sides.
So my heart, its course impéded,
Beats in my perturbed breast;
Doubts, like waves by waves succeeded,
Rise, and still deny it rest.

PATTY
Well, ma'am, as I was saying—

NARCISSA
Well, say no more of what you were saying—Sure, Patty, you forget
where you are; a little caution will be necessary now, I think.

PATTY
Lord, madam, how is it possible to help talking? We are in Barbadoes
here, to be sure—but then, ma'am, one may let out a little in a private
morning's walk by ourselves.

NARCISSA
Nay, it's the same thing with you in doors.

PATTY
I never blab, ma'am, never, as I hope for a gown.

NARCISSA
And your never blabbing, as you call it, depends chiefly on that hope, I
believe.

PATTY
I have told the story of our voyage, indeed, to old Guzzle, the butler.

NARCISSA
And thus you lead him to imagine I am but little inclined to the match.

PATTY
Lord, ma'am, how could that be? Why I never said a word about Captain
Campley.

NARCISSA
Hush! hush! for heaven's sake.

PATTY
Aye! there it is now. But if our voyage from England was so pleasant, it wasn't owing to Mr. Inkle, I'm certain. He didn't play the fiddle in our cabin, and dance on the deck, and come languishing with a glass of warm water in his hand, when we were sea-sick. Ah, ma'am, that water warm'd your heart, I'm confident. Mr. Inkle! No, no; Captain Cam—

NARCISSA
There is no end to this! Remember, Patty, keep your secrecy, or you entirely lose my favour.

PATTY
Never fear me, ma'am. But if somebody I know is not acquainted with the Governor, there's such a thing as dancing at balls, and squeezing hands when you lead up, and squeezing them again when you cast down. I'm as close as a patch box. Mum's the word, ma'am, I promise you.

[Exit.

NARCISSA
How awkward is my present situation! Promised to one, who, perhaps, may never again be heard of; and who, I am sure, if he ever appears to claim me, will do it merely on the score of interest—pressed too by another, who has already, I fear, too much interest in my heart—what can I do? What plan can I follow?

[Enter **CAMPLEY**.

CAMPLEY
Follow my advice, Narcissa, by all means. Enlist with me under the best banners in the world. General Hymen for my money! little Cupid's his drummer: he has been beating a round rub-a-dub on our hearts, and we have only to obey the word of command, fall into the ranks of matrimony, and march through life together.

NARCISSA

Then consider our situation.

CAMPLEY
That has been duly considered. In short, the case stands exactly thus—
your intended spouse is all for money; I am all for love. He is a rich rogue;
I am rather a poor honest fellow. He would pocket your fortune; I will take
you without a fortune in your pocket.

NARCISSA
Oh! I am sensible of the favour, most gallant Captain Campley; and my
father, no doubt, will be very much obliged to you.

CAMPLEY
Aye, there's the devil of it! Sir Christopher Curry's confounded good
character knocks me up at once. Yet I am not acquainted with him
neither; not known to him even by sight; being here only as a private
gentleman, on a visit to my old relation, out of regimentals, and so forth;
and not introduced to the Governor, as other officers of the place. But
then, the report of his hospitality—his odd, blunt, whimsical friendship—
his whole behaviour—

NARCISSA
All stare you in the face; eh, Campley?

CAMPLEY
They do, till they put me out of countenance.

NARCISSA
What signifies talking to me, when you have such opposition from others?
Why hover about the city, instead of boldly attacking the guard? Wheel
about, captain! face the enemy! March! Charge! Rout 'em!—Drive 'em
before you, and then—

CAMPLEY
And then—

NARCISSA
Lud ha' mercy on the poor city!

[Enter **PATTY**, hastily.

PATTY

Oh lud, ma'am, I'm frightened out of my wits! sure as I'm alive, ma'am, Mr. Inkle is not dead; I saw his man, ma'am, just now, coming ashore in a boat, with other passengers, from the vessel that's come to the island.

[Exit.

NARCISSA

Then one way or other I must determine.—
[To **CAMPLEY**]
Look'ye, Mr. Campley, something has happened which makes me wave ceremonies.—If you mean to apply to my father, remember, that delays are dangerous.

CAMPLEY

Indeed!

NARCISSA [Smiling]

I mayn't be always in the same mind, you know.

[Exit.

CAMPLEY

Nay, then—Gad, I'm almost afraid too—but living in this state of doubt is torment. I'll e'en put a good face on the matter; cock my hat; make my bow; and try to reason the Governor into compliance. Faint heart never won a fair lady.

SONG.

Why should I vain fears discover,
Prove a dying, sighing swain?
Why turn shilly-shally lover,
Only to prolong my pain?
When we woo the dear enslaver,
Boldly ask, and she will grant;
How should we obtain a favour,
But by telling what we want?

[Enter **TRUDGE** and **WOWSKI**, (as from the ship), with a dirty **RUNNER** to one of the inns.

RUNNER
This way, sir; if you will let me recommend—

TRUDGE
Come along, Wows! Take care of your furs, and your feathers, my girl!

WOWSKI
Iss.

TRUDGE
That's right.—Somebody might steal 'em, perhaps.

WOWSKI
Steal!—What that?

TRUDGE
Oh Lord! see what one loses by not being born in a christian country.

RUNNER
If you would, sir, but mention to your master, the house that belongs to my master; the best accommodations on the quay.—

TRUDGE
What's your sign, my lad?

RUNNER
The Crown, sir.—Here it is.

TRUDGE
Well, get us a room for half an hour, and we'll come: and harkee! let it be light and airy, d'ye hear? My master has been used to your open apartments lately.

RUNNER
Depend on it.—Much obliged to you, sir.

[Exit.

WOWSKI
Who be that fine man? He great prince?

TRUDGE
A prince—Ha! ha!—No, not quite a prince—but he belongs to the Crown. But how do you like this, Wows? Isn't it fine?

WOWSKI
Wonder!

TRUDGE
Fine men, eh?

WOWSKI
Iss! all white; like you.

TRUDGE
Yes, all the fine men are like me. As different from your people as powder and ink, or paper and blacking.

WOWSKI
And fine lady—Face like snow.

TRUDGE
What! the fine lady's complexions? Oh, yes, exactly; for too much heat very often dissolves 'em! Then their dress, too.

WOWSKI
Your countrymen dress so?

TRUDGE
Better, better a great deal. Why, a young flashy Englishman will sometimes carry a whole fortune on his back. But did you mind the women? All here—and there;—

[Pointing before and behind.

—they have it all from us in England.—And then the fine things they carry on their heads, Wowski.

WOWSKI

Iss. One lady carry good fish—so fine, she call every body to look at her.

TRUDGE

Pshaw! an old woman bawling flounders. But the fine girls we meet, here, on the quay—so round and so plump!

WOWSKI

You not love me now?

TRUDGE

Not love you! Zounds, have not I given you proofs?

WOWSKI

Iss. Great many: but now you get here, you forget poor Wowski!

TRUDGE

Not I. I'll stick to you like wax.

WOWSKI

Ah! I fear! What make you love me now?

TRUDGE

Gratitude, to be sure.

WOWSKI

What that?

TRUDGE

Ha! this it is, now, to live without education. The poor dull devils of her country are all in the practice of gratitude, without finding out what it means; while we can tell the meaning of it, with little or no practice at all.—Lord, Lord, what a fine advantage christian learning is! Hark'ee, Wows!

WOWSKI

Iss.

TRUDGE

Now we've accomplished our landing, I'll accomplish you. You remember the instructions I gave you on the voyage?

WOWSKI
Iss.

TRUDGE
Let's see now—What are you to do, when I introduce you to the nobility, gentry, and others—of my acquaintance?

WOWSKI
Make believe sit down; then get up.

TRUDGE
Let me see you do it.

[She makes a low courtesy.

Very well! and how are you to recommend yourself, when you have nothing to say, amongst all our great friends?

WOWSKI
Grin—show my teeth.

TRUDGE
Right! they'll think you've lived with people of fashion. But suppose you meet an old shabby friend in misfortune, that you don't wish to be seen speak to—what would you do?

WOWSKI
Look blind—not see him.

TRUDGE
Why would you do that?

WOWSKI
'Cause I can't see good friend in distress.

TRUDGE

That's a good girl! and I wish every body could boast of so kind a motive for such cursed cruel behaviour.—Lord! how some of your flashy bankers' clerks have cut me in Threadneedle street.—But come, though we have got among fine folks, here, in an English settlement, I won't be ashamed of my old acquaintance: yet, for my own part, I should not be sorry, now, to see my old friend with a new face.—Odsbobs! I see Mr. Inkle—Go in, Wows; call for what you like best.

WOWSKI
Then I call for you—ah! I fear I not see you often now. But you come soon—

SONG.
Remember when we walked alone,
And heard, so gruff, the lion growl:
And when the moon so bright it shone,
We saw the wolf look up and howl;
I led you well, safe to our cell,
While tremblingly,
You said to me,
—And kiss'd so sweet—dear Wowski tell,
How could I live without ye?
But now you come across the sea,
And tell me here no monsters roar;
You'll walk alone, and leave poor me,
When wolves, to fright you, howl no more.
But ah! think well on our old cell,
Where tremblingly,
You kiss'd poor me—
Perhaps you'll say—dear Wowski tell,
How can I live without ye?

[Exit **WOWSKI**.

TRUDGE
Who have we here?

[Enter **1ST PLANTER**.

1ST PLANTER

Hark'ee, young man! Is that young Indian of yours going to our market?

TRUDGE
Not she—she never went to market in all her life.

1ST PLANTER
I mean, is she for our sale of slaves? Our black fair?

TRUDGE
A black fair, ha! ha! ha! You hold it on a brown green, I suppose.

1ST PLANTER
She's your slave, I take it?

TRUDGE
Yes; and I'm her humble servant, I take it.

1ST PLANTER
Aye, aye, natural enough at sea.—But at how much do you value her?

TRUDGE
Just as much as she has saved me—My own life.

1ST PLANTER
Pshaw! you mean to sell her?

TRUDGE [Staring]
Zounds! what a devil of a fellow! Sell Wows!—my poor, dear, dingy, wife!

1ST PLANTER
Come, come, I've heard your story from the ship.—Don't let's haggle; I'll bid as fair as any trader amongst us. But no tricks upon travellers, young man, to raise your price.—Your wife, indeed! Why she's no christian!

TRUDGE
No; but I am; so I shall do as I'd be done by: and, if you were a good one yourself, you'd know, that fellow-feeling for a poor body, who wants your help, is the noblest mark of our religion.—I wou'dn't be articled clerk to such a fellow for the world.

1ST PLANTER

Hey-day! the booby's in love with her! Why, sure, friend, you would not live here with a black?

TRUDGE

Plague on't; there it is. I shall be laughed out of my honesty, here.—But you may be jogging, friend; I may feel a little queer, perhaps, at showing her face—but, dam me, if ever I do any thing to make me asham'd of showing my own.

1ST PLANTER

Why, I tell you, her very complexion—

TRUDGE

Rot her complexion—I'll tell you what, Mr. Fair-trader, if your head and heart were to change places, I've a notion you'd be as black in the face as an ink-bottle.

1ST PLANTER

Pshaw! the fellow's a fool—a rude rascal—he ought to be sent back to the savages again. He's not fit to live among us christians.

[Exit **1ST PLANTER**.

TRUDGE

Oh, here comes my master, at last.

[Enter **INKLE**, and a **2ND PLANTER**.

INKLE

Nay, sir, I understand your customs well; your Indian markets are not unknown to me.

2ND PLANTER

And, as you seem to understand business, I need not tell you, that dispatch is the soul of it. Her name you say is—

INKLE

Yarico: but urge this no more, I beg you; I must not listen to it: for, to speak freely, her anxious care of me demands, that here,—though here it may seem strange—I should avow my love for her.

2ND PLANTER
Lord help you for a merchant!—It's the first time I ever heard a trader talk of love; except, indeed, the love of trade, and the love of the Sweet Molly, my ship.

INKLE
Then, sir, you cannot feel my situation.

2ND PLANTER
Oh yes, I can! we have a hundred such cases just after a voyage; but they never last long on land. It's amazing how constant a young man is in a ship! But, in two words, will you dispose of her, or no?

INKLE
In two words, then, meet me here at noon, and we'll speak further on this subject: and lest you think I trifle with your business, hear why I wish this pause. Chance threw me, on my passage to your island, among a savage people. Deserted,—defenceless,—cut off from companions,—my life at stake—to this young creature I owe my preservation;—she found me, like a dying bough, torn from its kindred branches; which, as it drooped, she moistened with her tears.

2ND PLANTER
Nay, nay, talk like a man of this world.

INKLE
Your patience.—And yet your interruption goes to my present feelings; for on our sail to this your island—the thoughts of time mispent—doubt—fears—for call it what you will—have much perplexed me; and as your spires arose, reflections still rose with them; for here, sir, lie my interests, great connexions, and other weighty matters—which now I need not mention—

2ND PLANTER
But which her presence here will mar.

INKLE

Even so—And yet the gratitude I owe her—

2ND PLANTER

Pshaw! So because she preserved your life, your gratitude is to make you give up all you have to live upon.

INKLE

Why, in that light indeed—This never struck me yet, I'll think on't.

2ND PLANTER

Aye, aye, do so—Why, what return can the wench wish more than taking her from a wild, idle, savage people, and providing for her, here, with reputable hard work, in a genteel, polished, tender, christian country?

INKLE

Well, sir, at noon—

2ND PLANTER

I'll meet you—but remember, young gentleman, you must get her off your hands—you must, indeed.—I shall have her a bargain, I see that—your servant!—Zounds, how late it is—but never be put out of your way for a woman—I must run—my wife will play the devil with me for keeping breakfast.

[Exit.

INKLE

Trudge.

TRUDGE

Sir!

INKLE

Have you provided a proper apartment?

TRUDGE

Yes, sir, at the Crown here; a neat, spruce room they tell me. You have not seen such a convenient lodging this good while, I believe.

INKLE

Are there no better inns in the town?

TRUDGE

Um—Why there is the Lion, I hear, and the Bear, and the Boar—but we saw them at the door of all our late lodgings, and found but bad accommodations within, sir.

INKLE

Well, run to the end of the quay, and conduct Yarico hither. The road is straight before you: you can't miss it.

TRUDGE

Very well, sir. What a fine thing it is to turn one's back on a master, without running into a wolf's belly! One can follow one's nose on a message here, and be sure it won't be bit off by the way.

[Exit.

INKLE

Let me reflect a little. Part with her!—My interest, honour, engagements to Narcissa, all demand it. My father's precepts too—I can remember, when I was a boy, what pains he took to mould me.—School'd me from morn to night—and still the burden of his song was—Prudence! Prudence! Thomas, and you'll rise. His maxims rooted in my heart, and as I grew—they grew; till I was reckoned, among our friends, a steady, sober, solid, good young man; and all the neighbours call'd me the prudent Mr. Thomas. And shall I now, at once, kick down the character which I have raised so warily?—Part with her—sell her!—The thought once struck me in our cabin, as she lay sleeping by me; but, in her slumbers, she passed her arm around me, murmured a blessing on my name, and broke my meditations.

[Enter **YARICO** and **TRUDGE**.

YARICO

My love!

TRUDGE

I have been showing her all the wigs and bales of goods we met on the quay, sir.

YARICO
Oh! I have feasted my eyes on wonders.

TRUDGE
And I'll go feast on a slice of beef, in the inn, here.

[Exit.

YARICO
My mind has been so busy, that I almost forgot even you. I wish you had stayed with me—You would have seen such sights!

INKLE
Those sights have become familiar to me, Yarico.

YARICO
And yet I wish they were not—You might partake my pleasures—but now again, methinks, I will not wish so—for, with too much gazing, you might neglect poor Yarico.

INKLE
Nay, nay, my care is still for you.

YARICO
I am sure it is: and if I thought it was not, I would tell you tales about our poor old grot—bid you remember our palm-tree near the brook, where in the shade you often stretched yourself, while I would take your head upon my lap, and sing my love to sleep. I know you'll love me then.

SONG.
Our grotto was the sweetest place!
The bending boughs, with fragrance blowing,
Would check the brook's impetuous pace,
Which murmur'd to be stopp'd from flowing.
'Twas there we met, and gaz'd our fill:
Ah! think on this, and love me still.
'Twas then my bosom first knew fear,

—Fear to an Indian maid a stranger—
The war-song, arrows, hatchet, spear,
All warn'd me of my lover's danger.
For him did cares my bosom fill:—
Ah! think on this, and love me still.
For him, by day, with care conceal'd,
To search for food I climb'd the mountain;
And when the night no form reveal'd,
Jocund we sought the bubbling fountain.
Then, then would joy my bosom fill;
Ah! think on this and love me still.

[Exeunt.

SCENE II

An Apartment in the House of Sir Christopher Curry

Enter **SIR CHRISTOPHER** and **MEDIUM**.

SIR CHRISTOPHER
I tell you, old Medium, you are all wrong. Plague on your doubts! Inkle shall have my Narcissa. Poor fellow! I dare say he's finely chagrined at this temporary parting—Eat up with the blue devils, I warrant.

MEDIUM
Eat up by the black devils, I warrant; for I left him in hellish hungry company.

SIR CHRISTOPHER
Pshaw! he'll arrive with the next vessel, depend on't—besides, have not I had this in view ever since they were children? I must and will have it so, I tell you. Is not it, as it were, a marriage made above? They shall meet, I'm positive.

MEDIUM
Shall they? Then they must meet where the marriage was made; for hang me, if I think it will ever happen below.

SIR CHRISTOPHER
Ha!—and if that is the case—hang me, if I think you'll ever be at the celebration of it.

MEDIUM
Yet, let me tell you, Sir Christopher Curry, my character is as unsullied as a sheet of white paper.

SIR CHRISTOPHER
Well said, old fool's-cap! and it's as mere a blank as a sheet of white paper. You are honest, old Medium, by comparison, just as a fellow sentenced to transportation is happier than his companion condemned to the gallows—Very worthy, because you are no rogue; tender hearted, because you never go to fires and executions; and an affectionate father and husband, because you never pinch your children, or kick your wife out of bed.

MEDIUM
And that, as the world goes, is more than every man can say for himself. Yet, since you force me to speak my positive qualities—but, no matter,— you remember me in London; didn't I, as member of the Humane Society, bring a man out of the New River, who, it was afterwards found, had done me an injury?

SIR CHRISTOPHER
And, dam'me, if I would not kick any man into the New River that had done me an injury. There's the difference of our honesty. Oons! if you want to be an honest fellow, act from the impulse of nature. Why, you have no more gall than a pigeon.

MEDIUM
And you have as much gall as a turkey cock, and are as hot into the bargain—You're always so hasty; among the hodge-podge of your foibles, passion is always predominant.

SIR CHRISTOPHER
So much the better.—Foibles, quotha? foibles are foils that give additional lustre to the gems of virtue. You have not so many foils as I, perhaps.

MEDIUM
And, what's more, I don't want 'em, Sir Christopher, I thank you.

SIR CHRISTOPHER
Very true; for the devil a gem have you to set off with 'em.

MEDIUM
Well, well; I never mention errors; that, I flatter myself, is no disagreeable quality.—It don't become me to say you are hot.

SIR CHRISTOPHER
'Sblood! but it does become you: it becomes every man, especially an Englishman, to speak the dictates of his heart.

[Enter **SERVANT**.

SERVANT
An English vessel, sir, just arrived in the harbour.

SIR CHRISTOPHER
A vessel! Od's my life!—Now for the news—If it is but as I hope—Any dispatches?

SERVANT
This letter, sir, brought by a sailor from the quay.

[Exit.

SIR CHRISTOPHER [Opening the letter]
Huzza! here it is. He's safe—safe and sound at Barbadoes.
[Reading]
—Sir,
My master, Mr. Inkle, is just arrived in your harbour,
Here, read, read! old Medium—

MEDIUM [Reading]
Um'—
Your harbour;—we were taken up by an English vessel, on the 14th ulto. He only waits till I have puffed his hair, to pay his respects to you, and

Miss Narcissa: In the mean time, he has ordered me to brush up this letter for your honour, from
Your humble Servant, to command,
Timothy Trudge.

SIR CHRISTOPHER
Hey day! Here's a style! the voyage has jumbled the fellow's brains out of their places; the water has made his head turn round. But no matter; mine turns round, too. I'll go and prepare Narcissa directly; they shall be married slap-dash, as soon as he comes from the quay. From Neptune to Hymen: from the hammock to the bridal bed—Ha! old boy!

MEDIUM
Well, well; don't flurry yourself—you're so hot!

SIR CHRISTOPHER
Hot! blood, ar'n't I in the West Indies? Ar'n't I governor of Barbadoes? He shall have her as soon as he sets his foot on shore. "But, plague on't, he's so slow."—She shall rise to him like Venus out of the sea. His hair puffed? He ought to have been puffing, here, out of breath, by this time.

MEDIUM
Very true; but Venus's husband is always supposed to be lame, you know, Sir Christopher.

SIR CHRISTOPHER
Well, now do, my good fellow, run down to the shore, and see what detains him.

[Hurrying him off.

MEDIUM
Well, well; I will, I will.

[Exit.

SIR CHRISTOPHER
In the mean time I'll get ready Narcissa, and all shall be concluded in a second. My heart's set upon it.—Poor fellow! after all his rumbles, and

tumbles, and jumbles, and fits of despair—I shall be rejoiced to see him. I have not seen him since he was that high.—But, zounds! he's so tardy!

[Enter **SERVANT**.

SERVANT
A strange gentleman, sir, come from the quay, desires to see you.

SIR CHRISTOPHER
From the quay? Od's my life!—'Tis he—'Tis Inkle! Show him up directly.

[Exit **SERVANT**.

The rogue is expeditious after all.—I'm so happy.

[Enter **CAMPLEY**.

My dear fellow!

[Shakes hands.

I'm rejoiced to see you. Welcome; welcome here, with all my soul!

CAMPLEY
This reception, Sir Christopher, is beyond my warmest wishes—Unknown to you—

SIR CHRISTOPHER
Aye, aye; we shall be better acquainted by and by. Well, and how, eh! tell me!—But old Medium and I have talked over your affair a hundred times a day, ever since Narcissa arrived.

CAMPLEY
You surprise me! Are you then really acquainted with the whole affair?

SIR CHRISTOPHER
Every tittle.

CAMPLEY
And, can you, sir, pardon what is past?—

SIR CHRISTOPHER
Pooh! how could you help it?

CAMPLEY
Very true—sailing in the same ship—and—But when you consider the past state of my mind—the black prospect before me.—

SIR CHRISTOPHER
Ha! ha! Black enough, I dare say.

CAMPLEY
The difficulty I have felt in bringing myself face to face to you.

SIR CHRISTOPHER
That I am convinced of—but I knew you would come the first opportunity.

CAMPLEY
Very true: yet the distance between the Governor of Barbadoes and myself.

[Bowing.

SIR CHRISTOPHER
Yes—a devilish way asunder.

CAMPLEY
Granted, sir: which has distressed me with the cruellest doubts as to our meeting.

SIR CHRISTOPHER
It was a toss up.

CAMPLEY
The old gentleman seems devilish kind.—Now to soften him.
[Aside]
Perhaps, sir, in your younger days, you may have been in the same situation yourself.

SIR CHRISTOPHER

Who? I! 'sblood! no, never in my life.

CAMPLEY
I wish you had, with all my soul, Sir Christopher.

SIR CHRISTOPHER
Upon my soul, Sir, I am very much obliged to you.

[Bowing.

CAMPLEY
As what I now mention might have greater weight with you.

SIR CHRISTOPHER
Pooh! pr'ythee! I tell you I pitied you from the bottom of my heart.

CAMPLEY
Indeed! if, with your leave, I may still venture to mention Miss Narcissa—

SIR CHRISTOPHER
An impatient, sensible young dog! like me to a hair! Set your heart at rest, my boy. She's yours; yours before to-morrow morning.

CAMPLEY
Amazement! I can scarce believe my senses.

SIR CHRISTOPHER
Zounds! you ought to be out of your senses: but dispatch—make short work of it, ever while you live, my boy. Here she is.

[Enter **NARCISSA** and **PATTY**.

Here girl: here's your swain.

CAMPLEY
I just parted with my Narcissa, on the quay, sir.

SIR CHRISTOPHER
Did you! Ah, sly dog—had a meeting before you came to the old gentleman.—But here—Take him, and make much of him—and, for fear

of further separations, you shall e'en be tacked together directly. What say you, girl?

CAMPLEY
Will my Narcissa consent to my happiness?

NARCISSA
I always obey my father's commands, with pleasure, sir.

SIR CHRISTOPHER
Od! I'm so happy, I hardly know which way to turn; but we'll have the carriage directly; drive down to the quay; trundle old Spintext into church, and hey for matrimony!

CAMPLEY
With all my heart, Sir Christopher; the sooner the better.

[**SIR CHRISTOPHER**, **CAMPLEY**, **NARCISSA**, **PATTY**.

SIR CHRISTOPHER
Your Colinettes, and Arriettes,
Your Damons of the grove,
Who like fallals, and pastorals,
Waste years in love;
But modern folks know better jokes,
And, courting once begun,
To church they hop at once—and pop—
Egad, all's done!

ALL
In life we prance a country dance,
Where every couple stands;
Their partners set—a while curvet—
But soon join hands.

NARCISSA
When at our feet, so trim and neat,
The powder'd lover sues,
He vows he dies, the lady sighs,
But can't refuse.

Ah! how can she unmov'd e'er see
Her swain his death incur?
If once the squire is seen expire,
He lives with her.

ALL
In life, &c. &c.

PATTY
When John and Bet are fairly met,
John boldly tries his luck;
He steals a buss, without more fuss,
The bargain's struck.
Whilst things below are going so,
Is Betty pray to blame?
Who knows up stairs, her mistress fares
Just, just the same.

ALL
In life we prance, &c. &c.

[Exeunt.

ACT THE THIRD

SCENE I

The Quay

Enter **PATTY**.

PATTY
Mercy on us! what a walk I have had of it! Well, matters go on
swimmingly at the Governor's—The old gentleman has ordered the
carriage, and the young couple will be whisked here, to church, in a
quarter of an hour. My business is to prevent young sobersides, young
Inkle, from appearing, to interrupt the ceremony.—Ha! here's the Crown,

where I hear he is housed: So now to find Trudge, and trump up a story, in the true style of a chambermaid.

[Goes into the house.

PATTY [Within]
I tell you it don't signify, and I will come up.

TRUDGE [Within]
But it does signify, and you can't come up.

[Re-enter **PATTY** with **TRUDGE**.

PATTY
You had better say at once, I shan't.

TRUDGE
Well then, you shan't.

PATTY
Savage! Pretty behaviour you have picked up amongst the Hottypots! Your London civility, like London itself, will soon be lost in smoke, Mr. Trudge: and the politeness you have studied so long in Threadneedle-street, blotted out by the blacks you have been living with.

TRUDGE
No such thing; I practised my politeness all the while I was in the woods. Our very lodging taught me good manners; for I could never bring myself to go into it without bowing.

PATTY
Don't tell me! A mighty civil reception you give a body, truly, after a six weeks parting.

TRUDGE
Gad, you're right; I am a little out here, to be sure.

[Kisses her.

Well, how do you do?

PATTY

Pshaw, fellow! I want none of your kisses.

TRUDGE

Oh! very well—I'll take it again.

[Offers to kiss her.

PATTY

Be quiet. I want to see Mr. Inkle: I have a message to him from Miss Narcissa. I shall get a sight of him, now, I believe.

TRUDGE

May be not. He's a little busy at present.

PATTY

Busy—ha! Plodding! What he's at his multiplication table again?

TRUDGE

Very likely; so it would be a pity to interrupt him, you know.

PATTY

Certainly; and the whole of my business was to prevent his hurrying himself—Tell him, we shan't be ready to receive him, at the Governor's, till to-morrow, d'ye hear?

TRUDGE

No?

PATTY

No. Things are not prepared. The place isn't in order; and the servants have not had proper notice of the arrival. Sir Christopher intends Mr. Inkle, you know, for his son-in-law, and must receive him in public form, (which can't be till to-morrow morning) for the honour of his governorship: why the whole island will ring of it.

TRUDGE

The devil it will!

PATTY
Yes; they've talked of nothing but my mistress's beauty and fortune for these six weeks. Then he'll be introduced to the bride, you know.

TRUDGE
O, my poor master!

PATTY
Then a breakfast; then a procession; then—if nothing happens to prevent it, he'll get into church, and be married in a crack.

TRUDGE
Then he'll get into a damn'd scrape, in a crack.

PATTY
Hey-day! a scrape! How!

TRUDGE
Nothing, nothing—It must out—Patty!

PATTY
Well!

TRUDGE
Can you keep a secret?

PATTY
Try me.

TRUDGE
Then—
[Whispering]
My master keeps a girl.

PATTY
Oh, monstrous! another woman?

TRUDGE
As sure as one and one make two.

PATTY [Aside]

Rare news for my mistress!—Why I can hardly believe it: the grave, sly, steady, sober Mr. Inkle, do such a thing!

TRUDGE

Pooh! it's always your sly, sober fellows, that go the most after the girls.

PATTY

Well; I should sooner suspect you.

TRUDGE

Me? Oh Lord! he! he! he!

[Conceitedly]

—Do you think any smart, tight, little, black-eyed wench, would be struck with my figure?

PATTY

Pshaw! never mind your figure. Tell me how it happened?

TRUDGE

You shall hear: when the ship left us ashore, my master turned as pale as a sheet of paper. It isn't every body that's blest with courage, Patty.

PATTY

True.

TRUDGE

However, I bid him cheer up; told him, to stick to my elbow: took the lead, and began our march.

PATTY

Well?

TRUDGE

We hadn't gone far, when a damn'd one-eyed black boar, that grinned like a devil, came down the hill in jog trot! My Master melted as fast as a pot of pomatum!

PATTY

Mercy on us!

TRUDGE

But what does I do, but whips out my desk knife, that I used to cut the quills with at home; met the monster, and slit up his throat like a pen— The boar bled like a pig.

PATTY

Lord! Trudge, what a great traveller you are!

TRUDGE

Yes; I remember we fed on the flitch for a week.

PATTY

Well, well; but the lady.

TRUDGE

The lady! Oh, true. By and by we came to a cave—a large hollow room, under ground, like a warehouse in the Adelphi.—Well; there we were half an hour, before I could get him to go in; there's no accounting for fear, you know. At last, in we went, to a place hung round with skins, as it might be a furrier's shop, and there was a fine lady, snoring on a bow and arrows.

PATTY

What, all alone?

TRUDGE

Eh!—No—no.—Hum—She had a young lion, by way of a lap-dog.

PATTY

Gemini; what did you do?

TRUDGE

Gave her a jog, and she opened her eyes—she struck my master immediately.

PATTY

Mercy on us! with what?

TRUDGE

With her beauty, you ninny, to be sure: and they soon brought matters to bear. The wolves witnessed the contract—I gave her away—The crows croaked amen; and we had board and lodging for nothing.

PATTY
And this is she he has brought to Barbadoes?

TRUDGE
The same.

PATTY
Well; and tell me, Trudge;—she's pretty, you say—Is she fair or brown? or—

TRUDGE
Um! she's a good comely copper.

PATTY
How! a tawny?

TRUDGE
Yes, quite dark; but very elegant; like a Wedgwood tea-pot.

PATTY
Oh! the monster! the filthy fellow! Live with a black-a-moor!

TRUDGE
Why, there's no great harm in't, I hope?

PATTY
Faugh! I wou'dn't let him kiss me for the world: he'd make my face all smutty.

TRUDGE
Zounds! you are mighty nice all of a sudden; but I'd have you to know, Madam Patty, that Black-a-moor ladies, as you call 'em, are some of the very few whose complexions never rub off! 'Sbud, if they did, Wows and I should have changed faces by this time—But mum; not a word for your life.

PATTY
Not I! except to the Governor and family.
[Aside]
But I must run—and, remember, Trudge, if your master has made a mistake here, he has himself to thank for his pains.

[Exit **PATTY**.

TRUDGE
Pshaw! these girls are so plaguy proud of their white and red! but I won't be shamed out of Wows, that's flat.—

[Enter **WOWSKI**.

Ah! Wows, I'm going to leave you.

WOWSKI
For what you leave me?

TRUDGE
Master says I must.

WOWSKI
Ah, but you say in your country, women know best; and I say you not leave me.

TRUDGE
Master, to be sure, while we were in the forest, taught Yarico to read, with his pencil and pocket-book. What then? Wows comes on fine and fast in her lessons. A little awkward at first, to be sure—Ha! ha!—She's so used to feed with her hands, that I can't get her to eat her victuals, in a genteel, christian way, for the soul of me; when she has stuck a morsel on her fork, she don't know how to guide it, but pops up her knuckles to her mouth, and the meat goes up to her ear. But, no matter—After all the fine, flashy London girls, Wowski's the wench for my money.

SONG.
A clerk I was in London gay,
Jemmy linkum feedle,
And went in boots to see the play,

Merry fiddlem tweedle.
I march'd the lobby, twirled my stick,
Diddle, daddle, deedle;
The girls all cry'd, "He's quite the kick."
Oh, Jemmy linkum feedle.
Hey! for America I sail,
Yankee doodle, deedle;
The sailor-boys cry'd, "Smoke his tail!"
Jemmy linkum feedle.
On English belles I turned my back,
Diddle, daddle, deedle;
And got a foreign fair quite black,
O twaddle, twaddle, tweedle!
Your London girls, with roguish trip,
Wheedle, wheedle, wheedle,
May boast their pouting under lip,
Fiddle, faddle, feedle.
My Wows would beat a hundred such,
Diddle, daddle, deedle,
Whose upper lip pouts twice as much,
O, pretty double wheedle!
Rings I'll buy to deck her toes;
Jemmy linkum feedle;
A feather fine shall grace her nose,
Waving siddle seedle.
With jealousy I ne'er shall burst;
Who'd steal my bone of bone-a?
A white Othello, I can trust
A dingy Desdemona.

[Exeunt.

SCENE II

A Room in the Crown

[Enter **INKLE**.

INKLE

I know not what to think—I have given her distant hints of parting; but still, so strong her confidence in my affection, she prattles on without regarding me. Poor Yarico! I must not—cannot quit her. When I would speak, her look, her mere simplicity disarms me; I dare not wound such innocence. Simplicity is like a smiling babe, which, to the ruffian that would murder it, stretching its little naked, helpless arms, pleads, speechless, its own cause. And yet, Narcissa's family—

[Enter **TRUDGE**.

TRUDGE

There he is; like a beau bespeaking a coat—doubting which colour to choose—Sir—

INKLE

What now?

TRUDGE

Nothing unexpected, sir:—I hope you won't be angry; but I am come to give you joy, sir!

INKLE

Joy!—of what?

TRUDGE

A wife, sir! a white one.—I know it will vex you, but Miss Narcissa means to make you happy, to-morrow morning.

INKLE

To-morrow!

TRUDGE

Yes, sir; and as I have been out of employ, in both my capacities, lately, after I have dressed your hair, I may draw up the marriage articles.

INKLE

Whence comes your intelligence, sir?

TRUDGE

Patty told me all that has passed in the Governor's family, on the quay, sir. Women, you know, can never keep a secret. You'll be introduced in form, with the whole island to witness it.

INKLE
So public, too!—Unlucky!

TRUDGE
There will be nothing but rejoicings, in compliment to the wedding, she tells me; all noise and uproar! Married people like it, they say.

INKLE
Strange! that I should be so blind to my interest, as to be the only person this distresses.

TRUDGE
They are talking of nothing else but the match, it seems.

INKLE
Confusion! How can I, in honour, retract?

TRUDGE
And the bride's merits—

INKLE
True!—A fund of merits!—I would not—but from necessity—a case so nice as this—I—would not wish to retract.

TRUDGE
Then they call her so handsome.

INKLE
Very true! so handsome! the whole world would laugh at me; they'd call it folly to retract.

TRUDGE
And then they say so much of her fortune.

INKLE

O death! it would be madness to retract. Surely, my faculties have slept, and this long parting from my Narcissa has blunted my sense of her accomplishments. 'Tis this alone makes me so weak and wavering. I'll see her immediately.

[Going.

TRUDGE
Stay, stay, sir; I am desired to tell you, the Governor won't open his gates to us till to-morrow morning.

INKLE
Well, be it so; it will give me time, at all events, to put my affairs in train.

TRUDGE
Yes; it's a short respite before execution; and if your honour was to go and comfort poor Madam Yarico—

INKLE
Damnation! Scoundrel, how dare you offer your advice?—I dread to think of her!

TRUDGE
I've done, sir, I've done—But I know I should blubber over Wows all night, if I thought of parting with her in the morning.

INKLE
Insolence! begone, sir!

TRUDGE
Lord, sir, I only—

INKLE
Get down stairs, sir, directly.

TRUDGE [Going out]
Ah! you may well put your hand to your head; and a bad head it must be, to forget that Madam Yarico prevented her countrymen from peeling off the upper part of it.

[Exit.

INKLE
'Sdeath, what am I about? How have I slumbered! Is it I?—I—who, in London, laughed at the younkers of the town—and, when I saw their chariots, with some fine, tempting girl, perked in the corner, come shopping to the city, would cry—Ah!—there sits ruin—there flies the Green-horn's money! then wondered with myself how men could trifle time on women; or, indeed, think of any women without fortunes. And now, forsooth, it rests with me to turn romantic puppy, and give up all for love.—Give up!—Oh, monstrous folly!—thirty thousand pounds!

[**TRUDGE** peeping in at the door.

TRUDGE
May I come in, sir?

INKLE
What does the booby want?

TRUDGE
Sir, your uncle wants to see you.

INKLE
Mr. Medium! show him up directly.

[Exit **TRUDGE**.

He must not know of this. To-morrow! I wish this marriage were more distant, that I might break it to her by degrees: she'd take my purpose better, were it less suddenly delivered.

[Enter **MEDIUM**.

MEDIUM
Ah! here he is! Give me your hand, nephew! welcome, welcome to Barbadoes, with all my heart.

INKLE
I am glad to meet you here, uncle!

MEDIUM

That you are, that you are, I'm sure. Lord! Lord! when we parted last, how I wished we were in a room together, if it were but the black hole! I have not been able to sleep o'nights for thinking of you. I've laid awake, and fancied I saw you sleeping your last, with your head in the lion's mouth, for a night-cap! and I've never seen a bear brought over to dance about the street, but I thought you might be bobbing up and down in its belly.

INKLE

I am very much obliged to you.

MEDIUM

Aye, aye, I am happy enough to find you safe and sound, I promise you. But, you have a fine prospect before you now, young man. I am come to take you with me to Sir Christopher, who is impatient to see you.

INKLE

To-morrow, I hear, he expects me.

MEDIUM

To-morrow! directly—this moment—in half a second.—I left him standing on tip-toe, as he calls it, to embrace you; and he's standing on tiptoe now in the great parlour, and there he'll stand till you come to him.

INKLE

Is he so hasty?

MEDIUM

Hasty! he's all pepper—and wonders you are not with him, before it's possible to get at him. Hasty, indeed! Why, he vows you shall have his daughter this very night.

INKLE

What a situation!

MEDIUM

Why, it's hardly fair just after a voyage. But come, bustle, bustle, he'll think you neglect him. He's rare and touchy, I can tell you; and if he once takes it into his head that you show the least slight to his daughter, it would knock up all your schemes in a minute.

INKLE [Aside]
Confusion! If he should hear of Yarico!

MEDIUM
But at present you are all and all with him; he has been telling me his intentions these six weeks; you'll be a fine warm husband, I promise you.

INKLE [Aside]
This cursed connexion!

MEDIUM
It is not for me, though, to tell you how to play your cards; you are a prudent young man, and can make calculations in a wood.

INKLE [Aside]
Fool! fool! fool!

MEDIUM
Why, what the devil is the matter with you?

INKLE [Aside]
It must be done effectually, or all is lost; mere parting would not conceal it.

MEDIUM
Ah! now he's got to his damn'd square root again, I suppose, and Old Nick would not move him.—Why, nephew!

INKLE [Aside]
The planter that I spoke with cannot be arrived—but time is precious—the first I meet—common prudence now demands it. I'm fixed, I'll part with her.

[Exit.

MEDIUM

Damn me, but he's mad! The woods have turned the poor boy's brains; he's scalped, and gone crazy! Hoho! Inkle! Nephew! Gad, I'll spoil your arithmetic, I warrant me.

[Exit.

SCENE III

The Quay

Enter **SIR CHRISTOPHER CURRY**.

SIR CHRISTOPHER
Ods, my life! I can scarce contain my happiness. I have left them safe in church, in the middle of the ceremony. I ought to have given Narcissa away, they told me; but I capered about so much for joy, that Old Spintext advised me to go and cool my heels on the quay, till it was all over. Ods I'm so happy; and they shall see, now, what an old fellow can do at a wedding.

[Enter **INKLE**.

INKLE [To the **GOVERNOR**]
Now for dispatch! Hark'ee, old gentleman!

SIR CHRISTOPHER
Well, young gentleman?

INKLE
If I mistake not, I know your business here.

SIR CHRISTOPHER
'Egad, I believe half the island knows it, by this time.

INKLE
Then to the point—I have a female, whom I wish to part with.

SIR CHRISTOPHER

Very likely; it's a common case, now a-days, with many a man.

INKLE
If you could satisfy me you would use her mildly, and treat her with more kindness than is usual—for I can tell you she's of no common stamp—perhaps we might agree.

SIR CHRISTOPHER
Oho! a slave! Faith, now I think on't, my daughter may want an attendant or two extraordinary; and as you say she's a delicate girl, above the common run, and none of your thick-lipped, flat-nosed, squabby, dumpling dowdies, I don't much care if—

INKLE
And for her treatment—

SIR CHRISTOPHER
Look ye, young man; I love to be plain: I shall treat her a good deal better than you would, I fancy; for though I witness this custom every day, I can't help thinking the only excuse for buying our fellow creatures, is to rescue them from the hands of those who are unfeeling enough to bring them to market.

INKLE
Fair words, old gentleman; an Englishman won't put up an affront.

SIR CHRISTOPHER
An Englishman! more shame for you! Let Englishmen blush at such practices. Men, who so fully feel the blessings of liberty, are doubly cruel in depriving the helpless of their freedom.

INKLE
Let me assure you, sir, it is not my occupation; but for a private reason—an instant pressing necessity—

SIR CHRISTOPHER
Well, well, I have a pressing necessity too; I can't stand to talk now; I expect company here presently; but if you'll ask for me to-morrow, at the Castle—

INKLE
The Castle!

SIR CHRISTOPHER
Aye, sir, the Castle; the Governor's Castle; known all over Barbadoes.

INKLE
'Sdeath this man must be on the Governor's establishment: his steward, perhaps, and sent after me, while Sir Christopher is impatiently waiting for me. I've gone too far; my secret may be known—As 'tis, I'll win this fellow to my interest.
[To him]
—One word more, sir: my business must be done immediately; and as you seem acquainted at the Castle, if you should see me there—and there I mean to sleep to-night—

SIR CHRISTOPHER
The devil you do!

INKLE
Your finger on your lips; and never breathe a syllable of this transaction.

SIR CHRISTOPHER
No! Why not?

INKLE
Because, for reasons, which, perhaps, you'll know to-morrow, I might be injured with the Governor, whose most particular friend I am.

SIR CHRISTOPHER
So! here's a particular friend of mine, coming to sleep at my house, that I never saw in my life. I'll sound this fellow.
[Aside]
I fancy, young gentleman, as you are such a bosom friend of the Governor's, you can hardly do any thing to alter your situation with him?

INKLE
Oh! pardon me; but you'll find that hereafter—besides, you, doubtless, know his character?

SIR CHRISTOPHER

Oh, as well as I do my own. But let's understand one another. You may trust me, now you've gone so far. You are acquainted with his character, no doubt, to a hair?

INKLE

I am—I see we shall understand each other. You know him too, I see, as well as I.—A very touchy, testy, hot old fellow.

SIR CHRISTOPHER

Here's a scoundrel! I hot and touchy! Zounds! I can hardly contain my passion!—But I won't discover myself. I'll see the bottom of this—
[To him]
Well now, as we seem to have come to a tolerable explanation—let's proceed to business—Bring me the woman.

INKLE

No; there you must excuse me. I rather would avoid seeing her more; and wish it to be settled without my seeming interference. My presence might distress her—You conceive me?

SIR CHRISTOPHER

Zounds! what an unfeeling rascal!—The poor girl's in love with him, I suppose. No, no, fair and open. My dealing is with you and you only: I see her now, or I declare off.

INKLE

Well then, you must be satisfied: yonder's my servant—ha—a thought has struck me. Come here, sir.

[Enter **TRUDGE**.

I'll write my purpose, and send it her by him—It's lucky that I taught her to decypher characters; my labour now is paid.

[Takes out his pocket book, and writes.

—This is somewhat less abrupt; 'twill soften matters.
[To himself]
Give this to Yarico; then bring her hither with you.

TRUDGE
I shall, sir.

[Going.

INKLE
Stay; come back. This soft fool, if uninstructed, may add to her distress. When she has read this paper, seem to make light of it; tell her it is a thing of course, done purely for her good. I here inform her that I must part with her. D'ye understand your lesson?

TRUDGE
Pa—part with Ma—madam Ya-ri-co!

INKLE
Why does the blockhead stammer!—I have my reasons. No muttering— And let me tell you, sir, if your rare bargain were gone too, 'twould be the better: she may babble our story of the forest, and spoil my fortune.

TRUDGE
I'm sorry for it, sir; I have lived with you along while; I've half a year's wages too, due the 25th ult. for dressing your hair, and scribbling your parchments; but take my scribbling; take my frizzing; take my wages; and I, and Wows, will take ourselves off together—she saved my life, and rot me, if any thing but death shall part us.

INKLE
Impertinent! Go, and deliver your message.

TRUDGE
I'm gone, sir. Lord, Lord! I never carried a letter with such ill will in all my born days.

[Exit.

SIR CHRISTOPHER
Well—shall I see the girl?

INKLE

She'll be here presently. One thing I had forgot: when she is yours, I need not caution you, after the hints I've given, to keep her from the Castle. If Sir Christopher should see her, 'twould lead, you know, to a discovery of what I wish concealed.

SIR CHRISTOPHER
Depend upon me—Sir Christopher will know no more of our meeting, than he does at this moment.

INKLE
Your secrecy shall not be unrewarded; I'll recommend you, particularly, to his good graces.

SIR CHRISTOPHER
Thank ye, thank ye; but I'm pretty much in his good graces, as it is; I don't know anybody he has a greater respect for.—

[Re-enter **TRUDGE**.

INKLE
Now, sir, have you performed your message?

TRUDGE
Yes, I gave her the letter.

INKLE
And where is Yarico? did she say she'd come? didn't you do as you were ordered? didn't you speak to her?

TRUDGE
I cou'dn't, sir, I cou'dn't—I intended to say what you bid me—but I felt such a pain in my throat, I cou'dn't speak a word, for the soul of me; and so, sir, I fell a crying.

INKLE
Blockhead!

SIR CHRISTOPHER
'Sblood, but he's a very honest blockhead. Tell me, my good fellow—what said the wench?

TRUDGE
Nothing at all, sir. She sat down with her two hands clasped on her knees, and looked so pitifully in my face, I could not stand it. Oh, here she comes. I'll go and find Wows: if I must be melancholy, she shall keep me company.

[Exit.

SIR CHRISTOPHER
Ods my life, as comely a wench as ever I saw!

[Enter **YARICO**, who looks for some time in **INKLE'S** face, bursts into tears, and falls on his neck.

INKLE
In tears! nay, Yarico! why this?

YARICO
Oh do not—do not leave me!

INKLE
Why, simple girl! I'm labouring for your good. My interest, here, is nothing: I can do nothing from myself, you are ignorant of our country's customs. I must give way to men more powerful, who will not have me with you. But see, my Yarico, ever anxious for your welfare, I've found a kind, good person who will protect you.

YARICO
Ah! why not you protect me!

INKLE
I have no means—how can I?

YARICO
Just as I sheltered you. Take me to yonder mountain, where I see no smoke from tall, high houses, filled with your cruel countrymen. None of your princes, there, will come to take me from you. And should they stray that way, we'll find a lurking place, just like my own poor cave; where

many a day I sat beside you, and blessed the chance that brought you to it—that I might save your life.

SIR CHRISTOPHER
His life! Zounds! my blood boils at the scoundrel's ingratitude!

YARICO
Come, come, let's go. I always feared these cities. Let's fly and seek the woods; and there we'll wander hand in hand together. No cares shall vex us then—We'll let the day glide by in idleness; and you shall sit in the shade, and watch the sun-beam playing on the brook, while I sing the song that pleases you. No cares, love, but for food—and we'll live cheerily I warrant—In the fresh, early morning, you shall hunt down our game, and I will pick you berries—and then, at night I'll trim our bed of leaves, and lie me down in peace—Oh! we shall be so happy!—

INKLE
Hear me, Yarico. My countrymen and yours differ as much in minds as in complexions. We were not born to live in woods and caves—to seek subsistence by pursuing beasts—We christians, girl, hunt money; a thing unknown to you—But, here, 'tis money which brings us ease, plenty, command, power, every thing; and, of course, happiness. You are the bar to my attaining this; therefore 'tis necessary for my good—and which, I think, you value—

YARICO
You know I do; so much, that it would break my heart to leave you.

INKLE
But we must part; if you are seen with me, I shall lose all.

YARICO
I gave up all for you—my friends—my country: all that was dear to me: and still grown dearer since you sheltered there.—All, all, was left for you—and were it now to do again—again I'd cross the seas, and follow you, all the world over.

INKLE
We idle time; sir, she is yours. See you obey this gentleman; 'twill be the better for you.

[Going.

YARICO
O barbarous!

[Holding him.

Do not, do not abandon me!

INKLE
No more.

YARICO
Stay but a little. I shan't live long to be a burden to you: your cruelty has cut me to the heart. Protect me but a little—or I'll obey this man, and undergo all hardships for your good; stay but to witness 'em.—I soon shall sink with grief; tarry till then, and hear me bless your name when I am dying; and beg you now and then, when I am gone, to heave a sigh for your poor Yarico.

INKLE
I dare not listen. You, sir, I hope, will take good care of her.

[Going.

SIR CHRISTOPHER
Care of her!—that I will—I'll cherish her like my own daughter; and pour balm into the heart of a poor, innocent girl, that has been wounded by the artifices of a scoundrel.

INKLE
Hah! 'Sdeath, sir, how dare you!—

SIR CHRISTOPHER
'Sdeath, sir, how dare you look an honest man in the face?

INKLE
Sir, you shall feel—

SIR CHRISTOPHER
Feel!—It's more than ever you did, I believe. Mean, sordid wretch! dead
to all sense of honour, gratitude, or humanity—I never heard of such
barbarity! I have a son-in-law, who has been left in the same situation;
but, if I thought him capable of such cruelty, dam'me if I would not turn
him to sea, with a peck-loaf, in a cockle shell—Come, come, cheer up, my
girl! You shan't want a friend to protect you, I warrant you.—

[Taking **YARICO** by the hand.

INKLE
Insolence! The Governor shall hear of this insult.

SIR CHRISTOPHER
The Governor! liar! cheat! rogue! impostor! breaking all ties you ought to
keep, and pretending to those you have no right to. The Governor never
had such a fellow in the whole catalogue of his acquaintance—the
Governor disowns you—the Governor disclaims you—the Governor
abhors you; and to your utter confusion, here stands the Governor to tell
you so. Here stands old Curry, who never talked to a rogue without telling
him what he thought of him.

INKLE
Sir Christopher!—Lost and undone!

MEDIUM [Without]
Holo! Young Multiplication! Zounds! I have been peeping in every cranny
of the house. Why, young Rule of Three!

[Enters from the inn.

Oh, here you are at last—Ah, Sir Christopher! What are you there! too
impatient to wait at home. But here's one that will make you easy, I fancy.

[Clapping **INKLE** on the shoulder.

SIR CHRISTOPHER
How came you to know him?

MEDIUM

Ha! ha! Well, that's curious enough too. So you have been talking here, without finding out each other.

SIR CHRISTOPHER
No, no; I have found him out with a vengeance.

MEDIUM
Not you. Why this is the dear boy. It's my nephew; that is, your son-in-law, that is to be. It's Inkle!

SIR CHRISTOPHER
It's a lie; and you're a purblind old booby,—and this dear boy is a damn'd scoundrel.

MEDIUM
Hey-day! what's the meaning of this? One was mad before, and he has bit the other, I suppose.

SIR CHRISTOPHER
But here comes the dear boy—the true boy—the jolly boy, piping hot from church, with my daughter.

[Enter **CAMPLEY**, **NARCISSA**, and **PATTY**.

MEDIUM
Campley!

SIR CHRISTOPHER
Who? Campley?—It's no such thing.

CAMPLEY
That's my name, indeed, Sir Christopher.

SIR CHRISTOPHER
The devil it is! And how came you, sir, to impose upon me, and assume the name of Inkle? A name which every man of honesty ought to be ashamed of.

CAMPLEY

I never did, sir.—Since I sailed from England with your daughter, my affection has daily increased: and when I came to explain myself to you, by a number of concurring circumstances, which I am now partly acquainted with, you mistook me for that gentleman. Yet had I even then been aware of your mistake, I must confess, the regard for my own happiness would have tempted me to let you remain undeceived.

SIR CHRISTOPHER
And did you, Narcissa, join in—

NARCISSA
How could I, my dear sir, disobey you?

PATTY
Lord your honour, what young lady could refuse a captain?

CAMPLEY
I am a soldier, Sir Christopher. Love and war is the soldier's motto; though my income is trifling to your intended son-in-law's, still the chance of war has enabled me to support the object of my love above indigence. Her fortune, Sir Christopher, I do not consider myself by any means entitled to.

SIR CHRISTOPHER
'Sblood! but you must though. Give me your hand, my young Mars, and bless you both together!—Thank you, thank you for cheating an old fellow into giving his daughter to a lad of spirit, when he was going to throw her away upon one, in whose breast the mean passion of avarice smothers the smallest spark of affection or humanity.

NARCISSA
I have this moment heard a story of a transaction in the forest, which I own would have rendered compliance with your former commands very disagreeable.

PATTY
Yes, sir, I told my mistress he had brought over a Hottypot gentlewoman.

SIR CHRISTOPHER
Yes, but he would have left her for you;—

[To **NARCISSA**]

—and you for his interest; and sold you, perhaps, as he has this poor girl to me, as a requital for preserving his life.

NARCISSA
How!

[Enter **TRUDGE** and **WOWSKI**.

TRUDGE
Come along, Wows! take a long last leave of your poor mistress: throw your pretty, ebony arms about her neck.

WOWSKI
No, no;—she not go; you not leave poor Wowski.

[Throwing her arms about **YARICO**.

SIR CHRISTOPHER
Poor girl! A companion, I take it!

TRUDGE
A thing of my own, sir. I cou'dn't help following my master's example in the woods—Like master, like man, sir.

SIR CHRISTOPHER
But you would not sell her, and be hang'd to you, you dog, would you?

TRUDGE
Hang me, like a dog, if I would, sir.

SIR CHRISTOPHER
So say I to every fellow that breaks an obligation due to the feelings of a man. But, old Medium, what have you to say for your hopeful nephew?

MEDIUM
I never speak ill of my friends, Sir Christopher.

SIR CHRISTOPHER
Pshaw!

INKLE
Then let me speak: hear me defend a conduct—

SIR CHRISTOPHER
Defend! Zounds! plead guilty at once—it's the only hope left of obtaining mercy.

INKLE
Suppose, old gentleman, you had a son?

SIR CHRISTOPHER
'Sblood! then I'd make him an honest fellow; and teach him, that the feeling heart never knows greater pride than when it's employed in giving succour to the unfortunate. I'd teach him to be his father's own son to a hair.

INKLE
Even so my father tutored me: from my infancy, bending my tender mind, like a young sapling, to his will—Interest was the grand prop round which he twined my pliant green affections: taught me in childhood to repeat old sayings—all tending to his own fixed principles, and the first sentence that I ever lisped, was—Charity begins at home.

SIR CHRISTOPHER
I shall never like a proverb again, as long as I live.

INKLE
As I grew up, he'd prove—and by example—were I in want, I might e'en starve, for what the world cared for their neighbours; why then should I care for the world? Men now lived for themselves. These were his doctrines: then, sir, what would you say, should I, in spite of habit, precept, education, fly in my father's face, and spurn his councils?

SIR CHRISTOPHER
Say! why, that you were a damn'd honest, undutiful fellow. O curse such principles! Principles, which destroy all confidence between man and man—Principles which none but a rogue could instil, and none but a rogue could imbibe.—Principles—

INKLE
Which I renounce.

SIR CHRISTOPHER
Eh!

INKLE
Renounce entirely. Ill-founded precept too long has steeled my breast—but still 'tis vulnerable—this trial was too much—Nature, 'gainst habit combating within me, has penetrated to my heart; a heart, I own, long callous to the feelings of sensibility; but now it bleeds—and bleeds for my poor Yarico. Oh, let me clasp her to it, while 'tis glowing, and mingle tears of love and penitence.

[Embracing her.

TRUDGE [Capering about]
Wows, give me a kiss!

[**WOWSKI** goes to **TRUDGE**.

YARICO
And shall we—shall we be happy?

INKLE
Aye; ever, ever, Yarico.

YARICO
I knew we should—and yet I feared—but shall I still watch over you? Oh! love, you surely gave your Yarico such pain, only to make her feel this happiness the greater.

WOWSKI [Going to **YARICO**]
Oh Wowski so happy!—and yet I think I not glad neither.

TRUDGE
Eh, Wows! How!—why not!

WOWSKI
'Cause I can't help cry—

SIR CHRISTOPHER
Then, if that's the case—curse me, if I think I'm very glad either. What the plague's the matter with my eyes?—Young man, your hand—I am now proud and happy to shake it.

MEDIUM
Well, Sir Christopher, what do you say to my hopeful nephew now?

SIR CHRISTOPHER
Say! Why, confound the fellow, I say, that is ungenerous enough to remember the bad action of a man who has virtue left in his heart to repent it—As for you, my good fellow,—
[To **TRUDGE**]
I must, with your master's permission, employ you myself.

TRUDGE
O rare!—Bless your honour!—Wows! you'll be lady, you jade, to a governor's factotum.

WOWSKI
Iss—I Lady Jactotum.

SIR CHRISTOPHER
And now, my young folks, we'll drive home, and celebrate the wedding. Od's my life! I long to be shaking a foot at the fiddles, and I shall dance ten times the lighter, for reforming an Inkle, while I have it in my power to reward the innocence of a Yarico.

FINALE.
[La Belle Catharine]

CAMPLEY
Come, let us dance and sing,
While all Barbadoes bells shall ring:
Love scrapes the fiddle string,
And Venus plays the lute;
Hymen gay, foots away,
Happy at our wedding-day,
Cocks his chin, and figures in,

To tabor, fife, and flute.

CHORUS
Come then dance and sing,
While all Barbadoes bells shall ring, &c.

NARCISSA
Since thus each anxious care
Is vanished into empty air,
Ah! how can I forbear
To join the jocund dance?
To and fro, couples go,
On the light fantastic toe,
White with glee, merrily,
The rosy hours advance.

CHORUS
Come then, &c.

YARICO
When first the swelling sea
Hither bore my love and me,
What then my fate would be,
Little did I think—
Doomed to know care and woe,
Happy still is Yarico;
Since her love will constant prove,
And nobly scorns to shrink.

CHORUS
Come then, &c.

WOWSKI
Whilst all around, rejoice,
Pipe and tabor raise the voice,
It can't be Wowski's choice,
Whilst Trudge's to be dumb.
No, no, dey blithe and gay,
Shall like massy, missy play.
Dance and sing, hey ding, ding,

Strike fiddle and beat drum.

CHORUS
Come then, &c.

TRUDGE
'Sbobs! now, I'm fix'd for life,
My fortune's fair, tho' black's my wife,
Who fears domestic strife—
Who cares now a souse!
Merry cheer my dingy dear
Shall find with her Factotum heve;
Night and day, I'll frisk and play
About the house with Wows.

CHORUS
Come then, &c.

INKLE
Love's convert here behold,
Banish'd now my thirst of gold,
Bless'd in these arms to fold
My gentle Yarico.
Hence all care, doubt, and fear,
Love and joy each want shall cheer,
Happy night, pure delight,
Shall make our bosoms glow.

CHORUS
Come then, &c.

PATTY
Let Patty say a word—
A chambermaid may sure be heard—
Sure men are grown absurd,
Thus taking black for white;
To hug and kiss a dingy miss,
Will hardly suit an age like this,
Unless, here, some friends appear,
Who like this wedding night.

CHORUS

Come then, &c.

George Colman the Younger – A Concise Bibliography

The Female Dramatist (1782)
Two to One (1784)
Turk and No Turk (1785)
Inkle and Yarico (1787)
Ways and Means (1788)
The Battle of Hexham (1793)
The Iron Chest (1796)
The Heir at Law (1797)
The Poor Gentleman (1802)
John Bull, or an Englishman's Fireside (1803)

Colman was also the author of a great deal of so-called humorous poetry (usually coarse, though popular) – My Night Gown and Slippers (1797), reprinted under the name of Broad Grins, in 1802; and Poetical Vagaries (1812). Some of his writings were published under the assumed name of Arthur Griffinhood of Turnham Green.